Continued Daily Sagas with Estherleon

~

Sequel to

Resolution: Tears of Joy - promise fulfilled

First Edition

ISBN 978-0-9987395-4-0

Published by Estherleon Schwartz

Contact: estherleon@estherleon.com
www.estherleon.com

Cover photo by Ivor Pyres
Back cover photo by Sara-Olivia Granberger
Front cover layout by Lionel Ochoa - zenceimagery.com

Book design and typesetting by Michael Rosen

Printed in the United States of America

Also By The Author:

Tears Of Stone and My Deal With God

Resolution:
Tears of Joy - promise fulfilled

Simply Meditate

Simply Meditate with Your Dog And Meow

Simply Meditate with Giggles

To my daughter, Carrie and my son, David…

Monday, June 19th, 2023 - 4:12pm

Really, for real, I mean really,
I proclaimed in my last sequel,
"I'm done." I wrote.
I said everything I felt
and sent it off to be published
and had my special day in March, 2023,
once again at BARNES AND NOBLE
at The Grove in Los Angeles
- a book signing.

"Yes, friends your gut knows best."

I called my best male friend, Ivor,
(he is worth reading about in my other books),
and told him, I think, I feel, I have to share
the experience at the hospital.
Once again that urge,
the chatter in my head
to share what happened,
may give maybe some comfort to some...
I am so grateful listening to my gut.

"the right thing to do"

This hospital, I mean, this major hospital
is considered as 'the best around the world'.
Back to Ivor, as he experienced
48 hours of me, sacred to death.
He said, "Esther, it's the right thing to do
to share your most intimate raw feelings
so others will relate and benefit.
I felt in my gut the words,
"the right thing to do",
is what really matters in so many ways.

"May the 'Source' continue to guide me."

So my friends, I will keep typing
as long as my fingers last,
as my thoughts go
faster than my fingers somehow,
like my other books.
This my friends, is a series of the daily sagas
that led to 'what really matters'.

Thursday, June 15th 2023 - 9:05am

Woke up and recited my thank you prayers
and for my soul returning.
You can look it up
under universal morning prayers…
Threw on my yummy warm overcoat
with a hoodie attached.
Tucked in my hair and put on
my dark shades and outlined my lips.
That's it…my morning routine
to head out 230 feet to Starbucks
and pet some waging tails,
you know what I mean,
en route to Starbucks like me,
of course after they pee and poop,
get a treat of their homemade Starbucks whipped cream,
licking it out of a cup.
So cute, I see the soul in dogs' eyes.
In fact, I see the soul in all animals.

9:15am

When I walk into Starbucks,
I get so much love from the baristas...
I am a bit of a pain in the tush (aka ass).
I like a pour-over, extra strong Pike's
with ½ and ½ pure milk,
steamed with lots of foam.
This is what they have to deal with...
me and they still give me my coffee
with a smile and bless me
to have a great day.
And I throw billions of kisses upward
and say "thank you, thank you, thank you"
and some shout out, "AMEN".

"Breathe, breathe, breathe Esther."

9:30am

Taking 3 zips of coffee,
I get my 'high'.
As I was taking my daily walk,
so happy in that state of gratitude...
So nice early in the morning,
no noise, just birds singing
and dogs wagging their tails and lots of
"Good morning, have a great day".
Out of nowhere, I started to get
some sharp stabbing pains
on the left side of my chest,
a tightening in my left arm
and my jaw and teeth felt very weird
and hard to breathe...

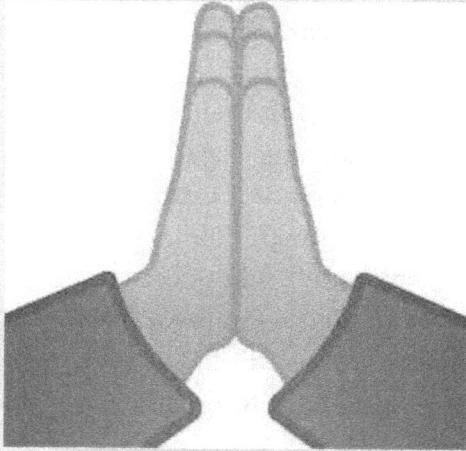

You see, back in October, 2022,
ready for this, I had a heart attack.
I was rushed to the hospital,
into the emergency room,
with a team of doctors
and a big light over me.
As I thought as you see in some TV shows
those electric pads they put on your heart
to revive you were staring at me,
as if they were saying,
"here we go"…
I pleaded with them
to first Face-time my kids.
They were all there
on the screen of my phone.
My daughter, her husband,
my granddaughter,
and 2 grandsons crying…
I said "I love you all,
do your very, very, very best
and let God do the rest"
as they were wheeling me into surgery.

11:30 pm

Waking up from a beautiful sleep,
I thought, "Wow, is this heaven?"
A beautiful man, a doctor
with a long grayish beard said,
"All good, you now have 2 stents."
That's all I remember
from that heart attack
except my son and Ivor,
looking down at me.

Thank God I had my cell phone and called Ivor
and in 20 minuets took me to the same hospital.
I did not want to call my son,
as I knew he would be more than shook up,
nor my daughter in Florida, so far away.
What could she do, even tho she is
a revered diagnostic practitioner,
mother of 3 children, 3 dogs, 2 are old and ill
and a non-demanding wonderful Argentine husband
and a tank of fish she feeds.
Is that not what a mother does,
always protecting her kids,
taking a bullet for them all…
I did not want to alarm her,
remember, she lives in Florida…
6 hours later she was at my bedside.

"...feel sad, yet hopeful"

11:45

So much attention was given to me in the ER.
I felt sad, bad, all those people
in the emergency waiting room,
throwing up, crying out for help,
feeling hopeless and their loved ones,
friends there with them feeling helpless,
until there name is called to be seen,
and maybe for some, too late.
Is this their destiny,
for your name after hours and hours to be called?
Is this their fate?
Look I am not 'miss goody two shoes'.
I think you know what I mean…

Just imagine, the emergency waiting room
transformed into a kind of
'House of Hope & Healing,'
rounded ceilings and stained glass
and artwork on the walls.
I wish I had the funds to do that.
All is possible when you want to believe.
And all pray together for each other…

3PM

**...I LIFT MY EYES AND HEART UPWARD
I SLOWLY TAKE A DEEP...DEEP WONDROUS
BREATH WHICH SUSTAINS ME**

I feel a Presence
a Calm that fills my being
I simply Inhale more deep wondrous Breath

My Soul, my Being is filled with wonder
Like the gentle stream
that flows and flows
Am I there?

As Calm as pure water, as pure as snow
All from Above
I am here in this mindful moment
in Bliss in Bliss in Bliss

I am Blessed

---

*When you repeat this at will, it gives power to the words
and they will serve you well.*

(*reprinted from 'Simply Meditate' by Estherleon)

Yet, once again and again in awe,
some deep "faith in hope" kicks in,
when your name is called in the waiting room,
to maybe determine one's destiny…
I will keep praying for you all.

Sitting, waiting to be admitted,
I was thinking about the presentation
that Ivor and I are almost ready
to bring to the world.
I NEVER SAW ANOTHER BUTTERFLY,
is about the children's drawings and poems
from Terezin concentration camp and found
TEARS OF GRATITUDE
after the Holocaust buried under rubbles.
I am a child Holocaust survivor,
I was spared.
I yearned to sing the divine prayers
when hidden in churches on the run.
When I became a Cantor later in life,
I so wished to become a voice for these children,
not to be forgotten.

The chatter in my head said
"no worries"

12:15 am

The EKG was negative,
but the pains were still there.
And the blood work showed something is off.
So there I was, on a gurney
in the ward against the hallway wall.
In a way I was happy to be just where I am,
not feeling alone and they give you a warm blanket
to feel cared for.
I made friends, was very comforting.
But, underneath that warm blanket
was me, 'scared'...
what the blood test and other tests
and pains in my chest could determine my destiny.
Wait, God, I need, I want
to finish this daily saga, this book.

...I never saw
another butterfly...

Children's Drawings and Poems
from Terezin Concentration Camp
1942 - 1944

I kept thinking about Alena Synkova,
one of the children from
I NEVER SAW ANOTHER BUTTERFLY…
part of our presentation wrote…
I met enough people
seldom a human being
Therefore, I will wait…
until my life's purpose is fulfilled
and you will come,
though there is anguish deep in my soul
What if I must search for you forever?
I must not lose faith,
I must not lose hope.

*"Ivor will make this a presentation,
I just know he will."*

Now every couple of hours
they tried to draw blood from my tiny veins.
I held my breath.
They tried so hard, until finally
they called a phlebotomist,
one who specializes in drawing blood.
The chatter in my head said,
"Girl, be grateful you have veins and blood,
you're alive, you're safe."
I kept thinking about the kids
in our future presentation.
I felt so proud to share the dark history
with the world.
Ivor did not really know or maybe he did,
how much this meant to me.
Only he, working with him for 20 years,
could make this presentation a reality,
never to be forgotten.

Maybe I was destined to have this experience,
this human cry out,
an inner gut pleading for wanting to live.
I often question myself,
"Why me, why was I spared?"
Who knows, maybe, to reminisce
memories and thoughts and feelings
of others of the past and present,
into another book and realize, "Never say never,"
as I wrote in my other sequel,
and now another sequel of the daily saga.
TEARS OF GRATITUDE

11PM

**...I LIFT MY EYES AND HEART UPWARD
I SLOWLY TAKE A DEEP...DEEP WONDROUS
BREATH WHICH SUSTAINS ME**

I feel a Presence
a Calm that fills my being

The Breath of Hope
The Breath of Faith

A Presence of Calm surrounds me

with Grace

with Wholeness

with Divineness

...You're home free

---

*When you repeat this at will, it gives power to the words
and they will serve you well.*

(*reprinted from 'Simply Meditate' by Estherleon)

Friday, June 16th 6pm

Lying here in the hallway.
witnessing life,
witnessing helpless faces,
yet the nurses and doctors
giving all of themselves
and me lying there,
looking up at the ceiling.
There is a sense of something,
something you feel
from your being,
saying, "I'm here, you're covered"…

An empty bed became available
up on the 3rd floor.
The nurses were so happy,
"Yeah, we got you a room,"
and hugged me.
I was feeling grateful,
yet kind of sad,
as they became like sisters
I never had.
I could talk to them anytime,
day or night
like I did with my brother,
who choose to be with God…
If you have siblings, cherish them,
and if temporarily not talking,
time has a way to heal the heart.

"Oh, oh"

As I was transferred onto another gurney,
I blew good-by kisses
and the elevator door opened…
In the past stays at the hospital,
when I was wheeled into my room,
they turned into a long hallway of rooms,
bright lights and into a private room
with a window and separate bathroom,
something felt weird.

11 pm

Off the elevator, they turned left instead of right
into a dim hall and buzzed into a dark ward.
Oh my God…
Flashbacks, people of all ages
being ordered to the left or right
was your destiny during the Holocaust…
At that moment
thinking about all those
downstairs in the waiting room.
Look, I'm not on any drugs,
it's memories I've lived with all my life.

And especially now, hoping
to finish our presentation of
I NEVER SAW ANOTHER BUTTERFLY,
and this daily saga, this book.
I must not lose hope,
as I am looking from the outside,
yet coming from my insides.
Chatter in my head,
"You're safe, you're in the best hospital in the world,
no left, no right, you were spared."
Esther, you are not in heaven looking down.

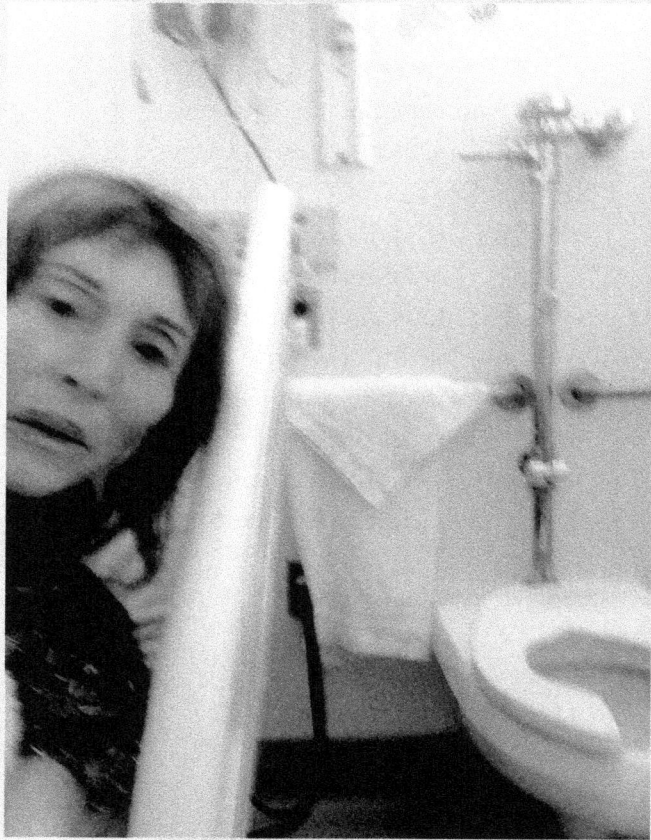

As I was now in the hands of new nurses.
They seemed nice, with a smile and caring.
There were about 15 separate cubicles,
surrounded with a curtain.
The nurse pulled the curtain.
All I saw in hysteria, a toilet next to a bed,
with a bright spotlight staring at me.
The nurse gently lifted me into the bed,
me feeling fear of the unknown and nothing familiar.
I could not believe how this bed felt and spoke to me...
In tears, I said, "This is the most comfortable bed
I have ever laid in, it's like magic"...
In the past, the beds I have experienced
were almost impossible to lay on.
My daughter always had to bring a crate
to put on top of the 1½-inch mattress.
There came in my daughter with the crate from Target.
She kept the receipt.

12 midnight

The nurses replied,
"Wow, people are always complaining
about the mattresses being so hard and bumpy".
With a smile on their faces
they welcomed me with some cookies
and said, "Your doctor ordered
a stress test for tomorrow.
Please eat the cookies now,
as thereafter you are on NPO."
That's all I needed to hear
to freak me out.
STRESS TEST.

This stress test is done with an injection
to speed up your heart,
as if you were exercising at the gym
peddling a bike like crazy.
Knowing this, I went
into a state of being
so scared like never before,
that I could remember.
I saw flashes of needles being put
in a child's heart for an experiment
and the heart protruding out of the skin.
I felt my heart beating so fast
and called for the nurse.
She took my blood pressure
and it was sky high.

"Thank you, God.

Thank you,
thank you,
thank you."

It's Shabbos, Esther,
the chatter in my head…
Sing, sing SHALOM ALECHEIM,
like you do so many times
when you wake up in the middle of the night
and your blood pressure is really high.
Remember, it does come down,
and I always say,
"Thank you God, thank you, thank you."
The idea of an artificial substance
to stimulate my heart,
felt like I was the experiment,
even tho it has been done
millions of times successfully,
to evaluate your heart
and fix what ever needs fixing
to continue to live…
another day, another day another day,
especially hoping to finish our presentation,
I NEVER SAW ANOTHER BUTTERFLY

*"Look upward, look upward.
Look upward"*

7 am

Already I'm trembling,
as they pull the curtain
and two transporters greet me
with, "Good morning,"
and check my wristband for verification,
is it you?.
Yes; it's me guys.
They are so up beat and polite and patient
and me so scared and holding the tears back,
plus my gown was all crumpled up
and I looked like shit.
They wheel me into the elevator
and wheel me out on the floor of imaging,
which happens to be the floor of the morgue...

In that moment, flashbacks of my life
are in my face, especially
when I do Shabbat and light the candles.
Especially when people
of all faiths and colors come.
Especially when they join me
in making wishes
and light the candles with me
and when tear drops fall
into the light of the Shabbos candle
and the flame does not go out…
And especially when my granddaughter
sends me a message from Florida
and says, "I love you so much Saftie
(grandma in Hebrew)."

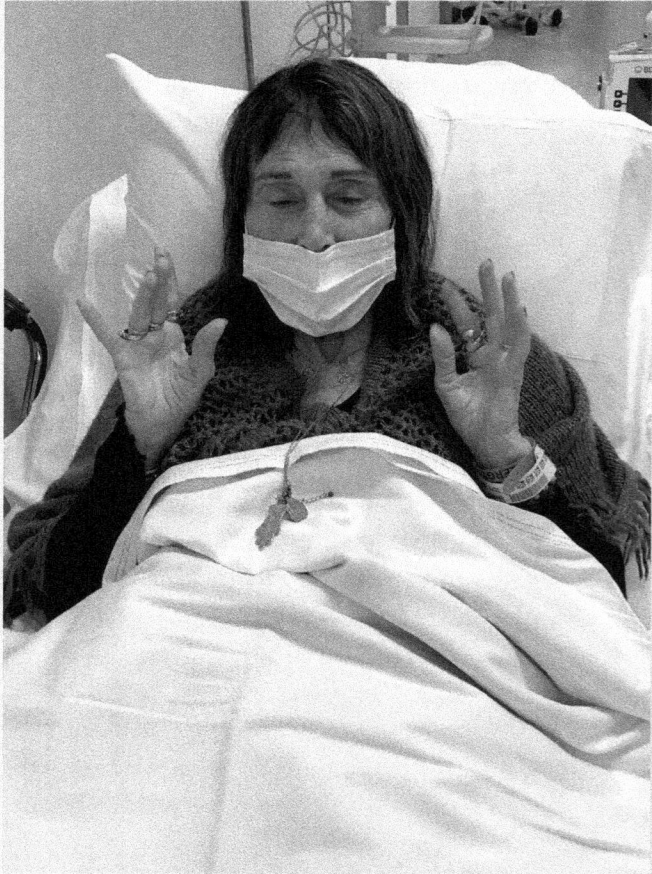

8 am

I am wheeled into a small room.
Two doctors and a technician staring at me.
The doctor with a needle in his hand
and a pen in the other hand
says, "Kindly sign this
for permission to do this procedure."
Me, trembling, and chatter in my head,
"Dude, I'm so scared, are you for real?"
Then he explains some of the immediate effects
of the injection that may occur,
like your heartbeat will speed up,
dizziness, nausea, but no worries,
the cardiac lab is next door for emergency...

...I LIFT MY EYES AND HEART UPWARD
I SLOWLY TAKE A DEEP...DEEP WONDROUS
BREATH WHICH SUSTAINS ME

I feel a Presence
a Calm that fills my being
I simply Inhale more deep wondrous Breath

My Soul, my Being is filled with wonder
Like the gentle stream
that flows and flows
Am I there?

As Calm as pure water, as pure as snow
All from Above
I am here in this mindful moment
in Bliss in Bliss in Bliss

I am Blessed

---

*When you repeat this at will, it gives power to the words
and they will serve you well.*

(*reprinted from 'Simply Meditate' by Estherleon)

I asked him, "Are people as scared like me
and just get up and leave?"
and he said, "Yes."
This is where God gave 'free choice'
now at this moment,
is my choice.
I so wanted to get up and leave.
Is this about faith?
Am I being tested by God,
my best friend,
who spared me from Hitler?

The feelings overcome me when I sing...

I feel I am with God,

  so safe...so happy...so everything....

    so good, so safe, so happy, so everything

A female elderly doctor came over
and held my left hand,
and touched the
Hamesch, the hand of God,
a necklace on my neck,
I never take off.
I signed the permission
and said, "It's Shabbos"
and started singing Shalom Aleichem
very slowly as the needle entered by veins.
The female doctor holding my hand joined in…

Toodley doo
I love you, too

I sang my way through
all the effects of the injection.
And then I heard
from all in the room,
"Hallelujah and Amen's"…

"Tears of Gratitude"

And the next thing
I was joyfully shouting
in the recovery room
in my bed, the gurney,
as folks were coming
in and out for the same procedure,
"Welcome, no worries, all will be good."
Sing your favorite song when they inject you,
sing it in 'slow motion'.
I did this for 2 hours…
I was as happy as a lark.
And went home in the afternoon
and started writing to all of you,
feeling it's the right thing to share.
TEARS OF GRATITUDE

So my friends,
"Never say never."
Like in my past sequel.
That's it for now.

-e

Hi, I'm back…
I really miss talking to you all…
So, here I am,
the daily saga continues.

My daughter and granddaughter from Florida,
have been here, in LA.
to witness all that happened in the last 30 pages.
They were going back in a few days
and said, I need a change of atmosphere.
Hmm, really, I love my space
that has a scared, peaceful vibe.
The whole exterior of the building
is a prayer garden.
Folks with children and dogs
are drawn to the butterflies of all colors
coming out of the earth
and welcoming signs
that I got at the 99 cents store.
Turquoise and soft peach,
reminds me of (hair pop colors I used to have,
more of that in my other books).
I sit every morning downstairs
on the deck, covered by a most beautiful
turquoise umbrella my son bought me,
and say, "Have a great day" to whoever walks by.
When you enter the foyer,
lavender and black tiles greet your feet.
Yes, this is a 4-unit apartment building
in a trendy area in LA…

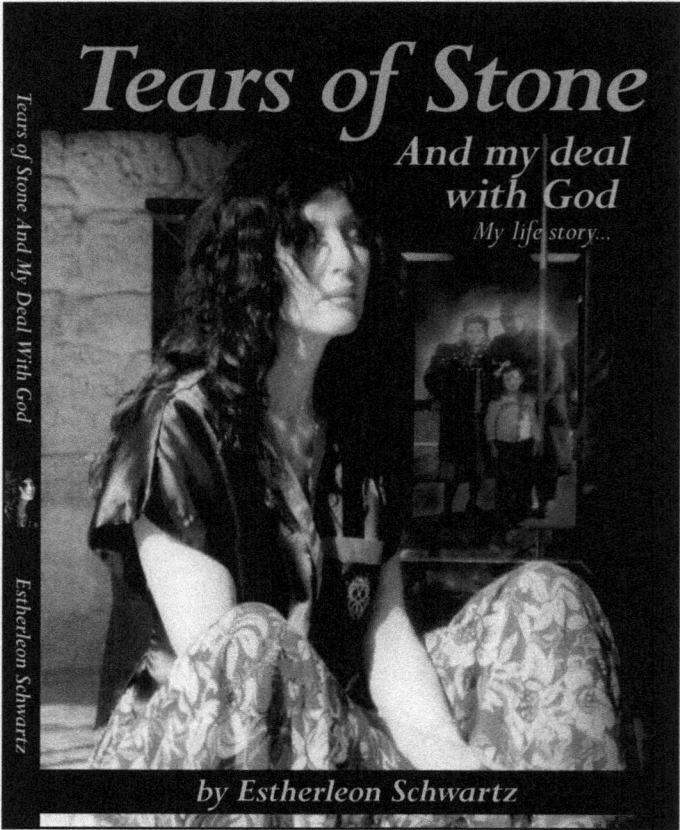

Tears of Stone

And my deal
with God
My life story...

Tears of Stone And My Deal With God

Estherleon Schwartz

by Estherleon Schwartz

Entering into my apartment
and walking up 18 stairs
carpeted in dramatic colors and walls of art.
It's kind of like entering into a fairy land of visual goodies,
that make you feel like Alice in Wonderland
and walls encased with hundreds of books
of authors sharing their take on life.
And some art (old souls) impressions,
from something like the West Wing,
at the White House...
Yes my friends, walls lined
with books of authors of all their stories
that speak to you...
In my first book,
TEARS OF STONE AND MY DEAL WITH GOD,
I share how books became my best friends,
as a child Holocaust survivor coming to America.

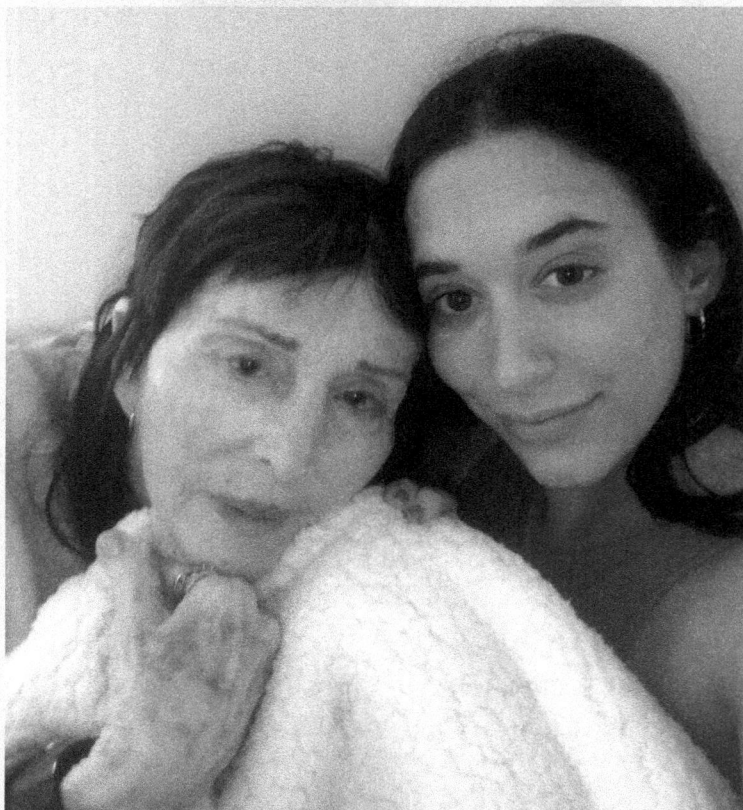

Continued…

I love being with my daughter and grandchild
and have not been on a plane
since my heart attack…
I packed very neatly
skirts and pants that match with tops…
And tons of other things.
Now we are boarding on American Airlines.
My daughter said they have new
comfortable seats that recline
and I can sleep my way to Florida
and soon see my loves,
Daisy, Kale and Emma, the dogs.

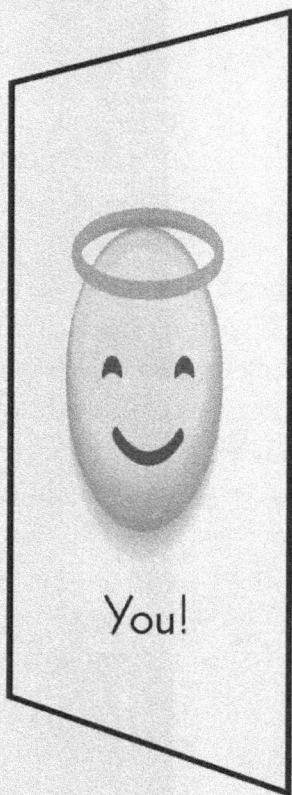

You!

Hey, I'm grateful, new seats on American Airlines,
wow… I tried to get comfortable in these new seats
shaped like sitting on a toilet seat without padding. …
I really, for one hour, tossed and turned,
like when a dog sniffing to do its thing
and finally finds the spot.
My daughter even brought a heating pad
that gave me some comfort.
Oh, at last, I found my spot, to rest my bones,
as I had lost a lot of weight.
About to doze off,
I was very thirsty and asked for some sparkling drink…
And the pretty flight attendant said, "Of course."
As I was taking my first zip,
the plane went into turbulence mode.
The whole cup of bubbly sweet drink spilled all over me
and the seat became its true destiny,
needing a plunger and bucket.
You know what I mean…

...to begin a beautiful new day

with meaning and purpose

Meow, meow
Woof, woof
We love you, now go on your way,
It's a Brand new Day
Hooray!

Love, your giggling buddies,
Hope, Grace and Angel

I was drenched, soaked.
My new bra, after 10 years I found, the wireless one,
the new bikini undies, just in case
I end up in the hospital again.
My granddaughter and daughter, looks on their faces,
felt like they were holding back giggling.
All I kept saying to myself, "It could be worse."
My suitcase was in the overhead, neatly packed
and TEARS OF GRATITUDE unreachable.
The flight attendant, (loved her hair color,
all in my other books, the hair stichk) said,
"Oh darling, are you ok?
Would you like some coffee, tea or Sprite?"
The chatter in my head, "Girl are you out to lunch?"
Oh, well the chatter in my head, "After all it could be worse."
Right, like my nausea saying hi and throwing up all over.
Yes it could be worse.
My granddaughter gave me
her oversized sweatshirt and pants,
as she had on lots of layers.
I found my spot again and woke up in Florida,
where you can touch the sky…
Kindly remember, this is a daily saga…

October 7. Saturday, 2023…

I'm searching for words to describe what happened…
As we were celebrating Shabbos, the Sabbath, breaking news…
Gaza terrorists took Israel at Gaza border
where Israeli settlements live, by surprise.
Hundreds and hundreds of Hamas terrorists,
brutally attacking innocent civilians
and slaughtering them to death in laughter…
I think for a moment the world stood still in shock…
This was not the usual sirens going off
and running to a bomb shelter…
As a child Holocaust survivor and seeing
and hearing the screams on T.V.,
I became glued to the news.
It was my friend, Destiny, in my book, *Resolution*,
a Silicon Valley brilliant geek,
kept sending me all updates on my phone.
You see my kids do not have cable
and very difficult to find the one news channel,
that may be biased.

I thought about what Anna Frank wrote in her diary…
"In spite of everything,
it's really a wonder that I haven't dropped
All my ideals."
Lying on the couch,
petting Cale, a Golden Retriver,
their dog that smiles and waggles her tail,
especially when you talk to her,
was dying of Cancer,
yet kept smiling and waggling her tail.
The vet told my daughter,
it was time, like now…

The next day, 9am,
a loving veterinarian's assistant came
with that little black bag,
and unzipped it…

My heart was so heavy
when I saw my son-in-law weep.
Watching Cale trying
to look up at everyone
and slowly her tail stopped waggling
and only sounds of whimpering and sniffing
filled the facing window
unto the sky so blue.

"May your memory be blessed."

The lack of her presence,
the bowl always filled with water,
the touch of her fur
and her presence,
her running up to you
after a long day's work,
those special moments you,
we shared...
Just sharing this with you all,
it kind of hurts.
I feel sad,
but
those memories,
I thank God for our memory...
for memories.

*"Sometimes I feel
I was a reinccarnted as a dog.*

May your memory be blessed."

Thank God for Dogs.

"Come on Ivor, lets have fun."

I got up this morning
and my phone and stared at me
with a reminder,
"Watch THE GOLDEN BACHELOR" new episode.
Right, I can't wait…
P.S. "That's a pun."
So I called Ivor and shared the good news
about senior bachelors for auditions,
and he said, "Oh, wow, I'll check it out."…
I told him what the deal is.
He gets to meet lots of senior women,
to have his choice.
Of course I suppose a prerequisite…
what they look like,
body style, and personality.
And he laughed as usual…
I feel, that certain laugh,
is kind of a nervous laugh
and I found the whole conversation
kind of amusing
and my feelings unexpected.

Really more about Ivor in my 1st book and sequel,
to understand him and me
and our friendship of 20 years.
Yes, he is a cute guy, great smile,
from India, raised in England
with that British accent
that is charming
and a beautiful pop singer
and on and on.
However it's his personality,
it...I am sorry to say it,
it "ssssu' s"... Ok SUCKS.
It just does not fit
his pure soul and loving character...

The saga continues...
The stages of my life,
or just maybe life...
Being a mommy to my daughter and son
even before birth and thereafter.
A revelation came.

When my daughter or son cries,
I, Mommy, feel needed.

Saturday, Shabbos, December 9th, 2023

The chatter in my head said,
"Esther, your kids are in their late 50's and early 60's, Ok".
So I'm not their mommy?
"Right, you are their mother
at this stage in their lives and yours.
Am I not still both at different stages?
When my daughter or son cried, "Mommy",
I felt needed.
Yes, they were young.
And loving friends say, "Esther, they're adults"
but for me they still are my babies
and I try to fix things for them
when I see and feel they need help,
something like that
when they're hurting or confused.

Thinking, thinking,
"What really, really matters?"

God really orchestrated everything
revealed in 'Divine time'...
My granddaughter was graduating
with a Bachelor's degree
in Business and Communication.
Four years of ups and downs,
but she did it and showed
those that rolled their eyes in the beginning...
Yes she had ADD, and all those other ADD'S.
I think people are gifted
when they have a disability
emotionally, mentally and physically.
I feel they are chosen by The Most HIGH
to inspire us to be grateful, to be thankful
and remind us, in spite of everything,
never to give up, keep truck'n,
stick with faith
and you will witness miracles...
In fact, it's written as a good deed
to say a prayer when
in the presence of that chosen soul...
Type in your computer or ask Siri on your phone
for "Miracles" and you will be so thankful,
sometimes more than not, we need a reminder,
do it. It works.
A blessing for Siri on your phone and computer
and your eyes, toooo.

And Dani also became a Yoga Guru…
'Conscious Yoga' developed into
worldwide most loved attended moments,
that turn into an hour that feeds
the soul and body with energy cheer, and hope.
And when she bends down
and looks into dogs eyes,
something magical happens,
when their eyes meet,
they lie still and just breathe,
a feeling that all lying on their mats,
the connection of 'the God-given Breath'.
She continues in her gentle voice.
Only sighs of gentle breathing
fill the room
with wonderment and peace.

Felt I was looking down from heaven
watching her 'do her thing',
an extension of me
to carry on in her own special way.
I felt such calm.

The manager of scheduling book signings
at Barnes and Noble in Los Angeles,
at the Grove is a very special young lady.
Her mindset to help community authors
in a cooperate world
was a gift to all unknown authors
and publishers and me.
Giving them TEARS OF GRATITUDE
like me, a chance to be heard,
giving them a chance to leave a legacy.
We became bonded with a special hug,
tears of joy filled my heart.
We booked a date in March 2024...

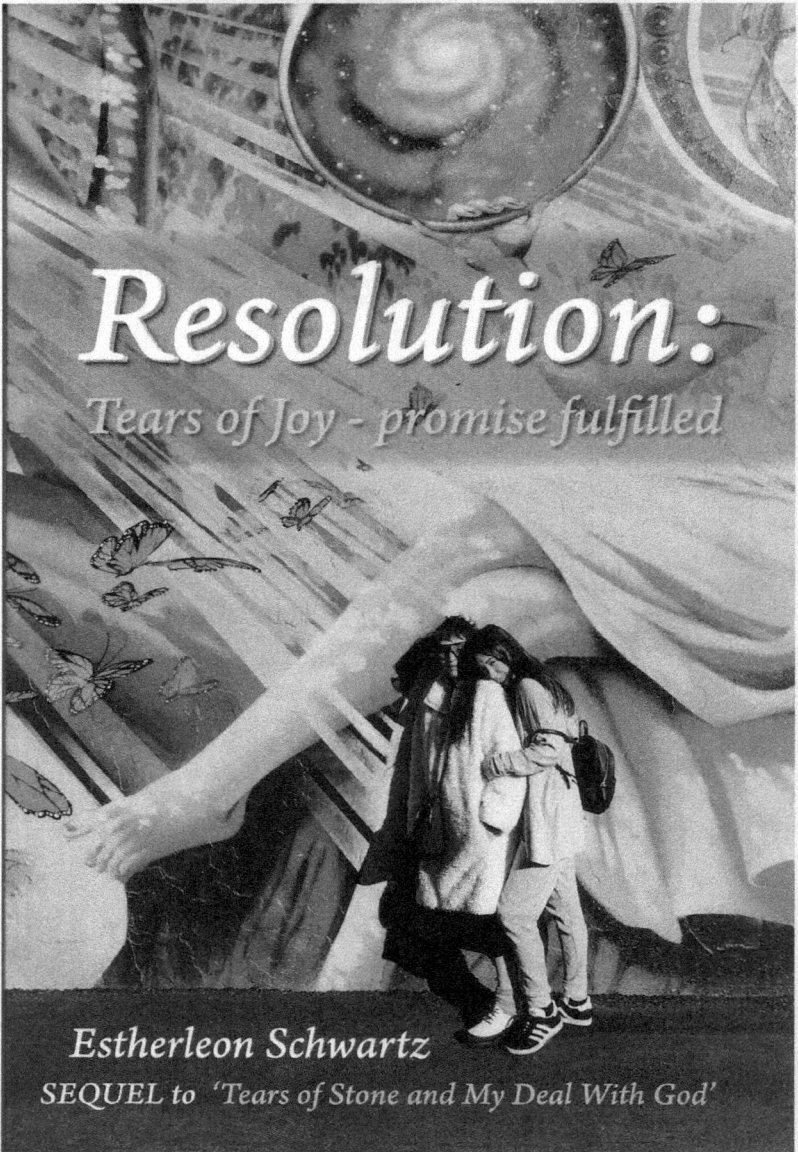

Resolution:

Tears of Joy - promise fulfilled

Estherleon Schwartz

SEQUEL to 'Tears of Stone and My Deal With God'

Living near the Grove,
I often take a walk there
just to watch people from all walks of life.
I just want to go where there is life and smiles.
I get a cup of coffee
and just sit and be...
I somehow see and feel people's hearts
and see waggling tails.
Maybe, as a child Holocaust survivor,
so much is dormant...
I just feel what I feel...
and am thankful I am still alive
to be part of this most beautiful God-given world,
especially after my heart attack.
More about that saga
in my previous sequel, *Tears of Joy*.

"Bless you, my friend."

As I am sitting here at my computer,
looking back at my life
and what really matters
and some people that cared,
I mean really revealed themselves
thru their actions,
even just in passing.
I feel at times people come
into your life for a purpose
Every morning I get a phone message
for the thought of the day,
which I never signed up for…
I developed an endearing, trusting relationship,
a friendship,
as his messages were so on
what really matters in this moment,
this hour, this day…
There goes God again,
looking after my heart, my being,
to start the day with a earthly divine mindset…
this unknown chosen messenger sends me…
God bless you…
P.S. his name starts with an R.
We have earthly angels…

I can't but feel so grateful
my fingers are writing what I'm feeling.
Really, is this me, getting down,
in black and white to be published
and maybe read by one
out there in the world...
I am thanking you, God,
for sticking with me all these years.
You just know when the presence surrounds you.
You see, God knows your heart.
Is there for you 24/7 in advance,
always, always, always...
And especially when you include the presence
in your daily ways... your life.
God is my best friend.

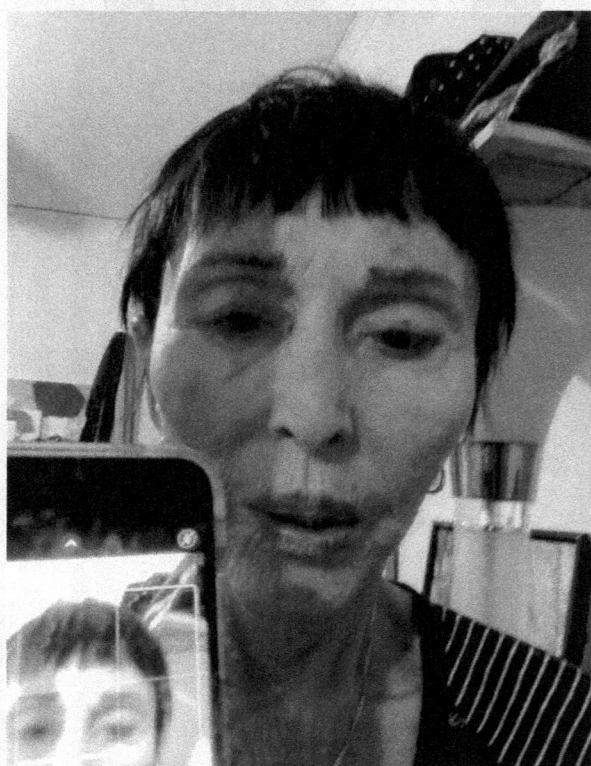

P.S. Back to my 'hair shtick'
as intertwined in all my sagas, in my other books.
My mother, early on, told me
to always leave my hair long
if you want a man
to look at you and have power
like Samson and Delia.
So my hair and hair color became
kind of my obsession until Janurary 1, 2024...
I waited in front of *Sirens Salon* for
Kristen, the owner, Sean, or Travis
to chop it all off.
I wanted the androgynous look.
I asked Siri on my phone the definition
and there it was.
That's me... partly male
and partly female in appearance,
having the appearance of both sexes...
wow, I feel I am a part of everything on earth.
With my hair chopped off,
reflects my deepest,
gut feelings about me and life.

Amen

believe...

believe...

believe...

I feel naked.
Yes, again I asked Siri on my phone
for an in-depth definition of 'naked'…
It replied, "Without the usual covering or protection,
the twisted trunks and naked branches of a tree,
blatant truth"…
I have always been in awe of nature
and felt part of the naked branches
and felt the wisdom of the twisted trunks
when I hug it tight
and love and fills my soul.
I am over at this point in my life,
82 years,
to finally let go of my mother's prophecy
of my 'hair power'.
I'm kind of sad that Samson
did not meet Joan of Arc,
look her up.

I want to, regardless of advice
to not talk about the current situation
in the Middle East since October 7. 2023.
People asking me what side am I on,
and how are you?
How can I be?
Those 2 questions hurt…
I feel for all God's people.
I pray for all people.
I hope you do, too.
One of my best friends, Destiny,
also asked me the same question,
"What side are you on?"
My response was the same,
and she, my Destiny, shouted at me,
"Esther, do something, do something,
they are murdering Palestinian babies…"
And we have not spoken since.

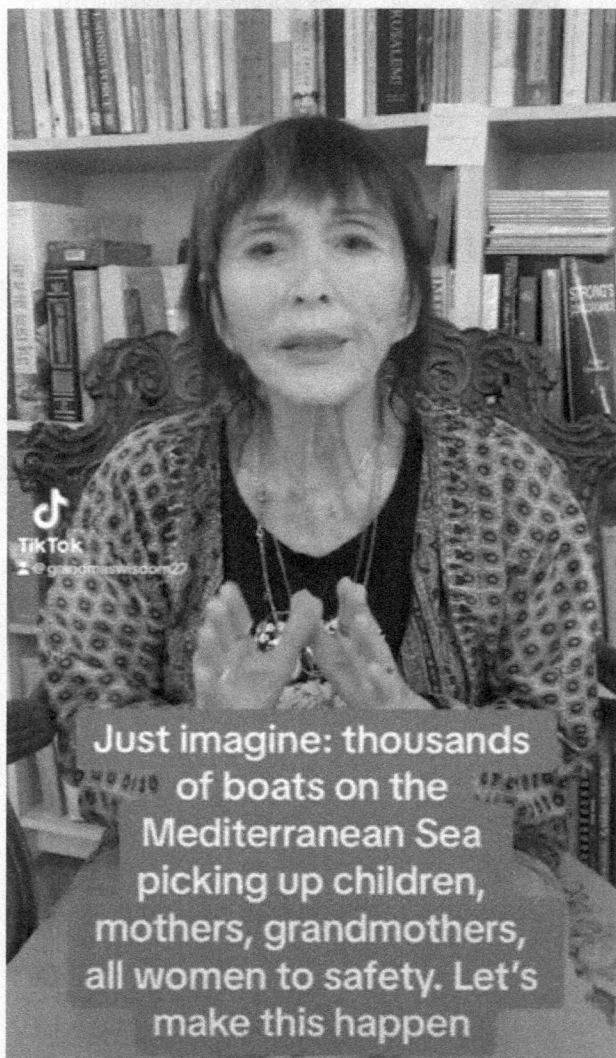

Just imagine: thousands of boats on the Mediterranean Sea picking up children, mothers, grandmothers, all women to safety. Let's make this happen

Destiny's words, "Do something, do something,"
haunted me day and night.
Me, born in times of slaughter
and now not trying to help in some way?
I am Esther who came to America
on the Queen Mary
with hundreds of Holocaust survivors
and holding on to my papa's hand,
me…made a promise to try to help in crisis
and in simple daily plights,
even if some said, impossible…

Since then, I started to really examine,
to reflect seriously,
what really matters,
I mean what really, really matters,
ESPECIALLY IN A MOMENT OF CONFRONTATION...

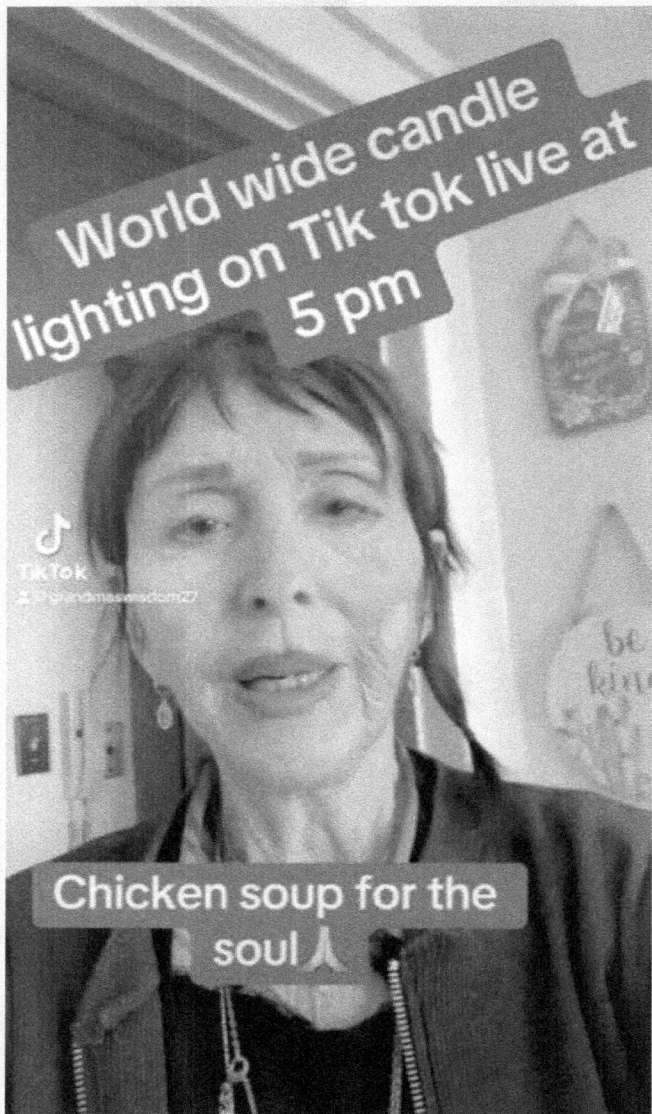

World wide candle lighting on Tik tok live at 5 pm

Chicken soup for the soul 🙏

I think I wrote about how my granddaughter
encouraged me to do videos
and go live on TIKTOK,
earlier, or in my other books.
What do I know about social media?
I am 'old school.'
Oh well, I committed
and she named me
GRANDMAWISDOM 27...

Your prayers count

Join the world in a special candle light for peace NOW!

And so yes, I reached out on TIKTOK…
SOS-NEED YOUR HELP-ASAP…
All this on October 7th 2023
on Shabbat…and me being confronted
and me, will do something.

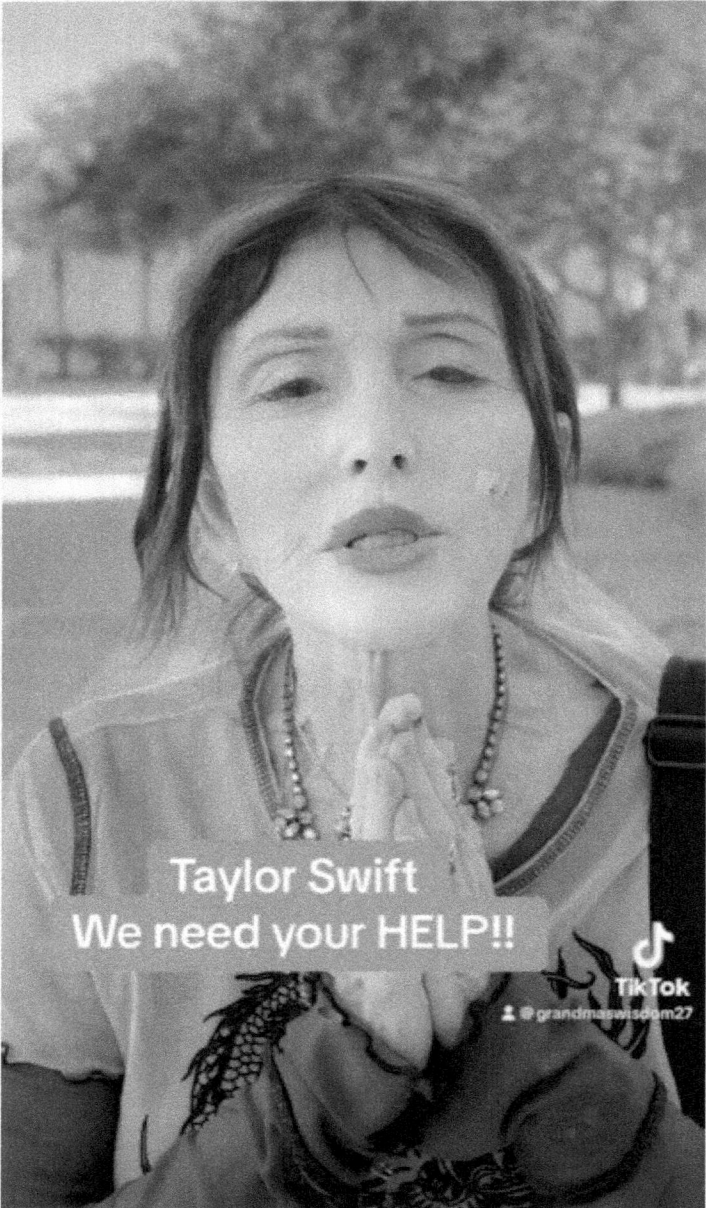

Taylor Swift
We need your HELP!!

I did videos on TIKTOK
reaching out to all people
all over world
to send ships, yachts, boats
to the border of Gaza,
to help get children,
grandmothers and women
out of harms way.
I even appealed to Taylor Swift,
as her bodyguard, I was told,
as an Israeli soldier went
back to Israel to fight.

SOS Animal Lovers

Dogs, cats, fish, birds they give peace and love. Elon Musk we need you to make that happen.

You see, my purpose and theme
live on TIK-TOK
was always and became a tradition
as a theme every week before Shabbat…
Worldwide Candle Lighting
for Harmony and Peace…
And that seemed to bring viewers
from all over the world,
mostly the young generation
to express how Harmony and Peace
can be achieved.
Bottom line, was, through their comments,
"We have more in common then not,
regardless of religion or culture
or what ever rainbow your face is."
This ½ hour sharing on Tik-Tok and Facebook
shined a light around the world
every Friday before or at sundown…
before Shabbos…

From: estherleon

Date: July 22, 2015 1:28:12 PM PDT
To: Kevin Brown

Subject: : KINDLY SCROLL ALL THE WAY DOWN: pat brown charter
school children.: A way to dispel..

History was made when one atheist argued that prayer in schools was unconstitutional and the Supreme Court agreed. Prayer in schools ended in 1962.
Now 2014, NOT the Supreme Court but the children have the opportunity
to make their own history by "repealing" that decision. Not by reinstating
prayer, but by starting a movement to replace it with a voluntary program of
beginning each school day with a Gratitude Circle before class starts, givng
each person to share what they are grateful for (as seen in video below). They
become buddies. One school at a time, and hopefully soon to be part of the
morning school curriculum all over the nation.

This will help dispel bullying,
discrimination and anti-semtisium.
Children become school buddies and
grow up caring and protecting one
another. Giving a child a chance to
express what they are grateful for in
the morning before class starts leads
to a good start for the day, gratitude
feeds attitude for the rest of the day,
for the rest of one's life. A simple
morale teaching tool that leads to "in
service work", to do good, instead of
joining gangs...a moment of reverence, of oneness.

I, Cantor Estherleon Schwartz, am a
face and voice, part of History and
have been invited to schools to share
my story of the Holocaust and how
I survived. My presentation is with
actual footage.. This is part of History. I will send you my bio.

Pretty please out there,
I need your help…
I have been calling for a meeting
with the superintendent of the LAUSD school district
regarding what I came up with:
The Gratitude Buddie Circle
to replace prayer, for a moral compass
to be taught as part of the curriculum…
when they took prayer out of schools
and did not replace it
with anything that gives a child
a moral compass…like teaching gratitude.

The Gratitude Buddie Circle
helps dispel hate and anti-Semitism.
Just imagine when a child enters pre-, pre-kindergarten,
after the pledge of allegiance,
each day, each child expresses
what they're grateful for.
They become friends, buddies,
as they realize they have so much
more in common than not.
The child that is shy and feels rejected
and may be bullied, and non responsive,
is the child that needs attention early on.
We cannot turn a blind eye
to the root of the problem.
Maybe this child feels rejected
and hate and anger dominates.
Their innocent soul does not know
how to deal with hate and anger...
And then at some point,
that tormented child
turns on his peers into school shootings.
No moral compass in secular schools anymore,
except in private schools.
I need your help to save lives
with petitions on social media, etc.
Thank you, thank you, thank you...e

REQUESTING A MEETING AGAIN

Begin forwarded message:

From: estherleon
Subject: Fwd: Hi Mr. Alberto Carvalho....GRATITUDE BUDDIE
CIRCLE TO BE IMPLEMENTD IN ALL SCHOOLS ...REQUESTING A
PRESENCE WITH YOU.
Date: March 29, 2024 at 4:51:02 PM PDT

Begin forwarded message:

From: estherleon <estherleon@estherleon.com
Subject: Fwd: Hi Mr. Alberto Carvalho....GRATITUDE BUDDIE
CIRCLE TO BE IMPLEMENTD IN ALL SCHOOLS ...REQUESTING A
PRESENCE WITH YOU.
Date: January 16, 2024 at 12:02:08 PM PST
To: superintendent

Begin forwarded message:

From: estherleon
Subject: Hi Mr. Alberto Carvalho....GRATITUDE BUDDIE CIRCLE TO
BE IMPLEMENTD IN ALL SCHOOLS ...REQUESTING A PRESENCE
WITH YOU.
Date: December 7, 2023 at 2:39:11 PM PST
To: superintendent

KINDLY SCROLL DOWN FOR MISSION STATEMENT.

gratitude buddie circle youtube main video

Begin forwarded message:
From: estherleon
Subject: Fwd: GRATITUDE BUDDIE CIRCLE TO BE IMPLEMENTD
IN ALL SCHOOLS
Date: September 7, 2016 at 3:39:11 PM PDT
To: newsroom

My solution fits in now as a story for all the right reasons...all good. Cantor Estherleon Schwartz. see what i sent you. e

School Board To Appeal Ruling That Banned ... - CBS Los Angeles
losangeles.cbslocal.com/.../school-board-votes-in-favor-of-appealing-
judges-ruling-that-banned-prayer-at-meetings
    Mar 7, 2016 ... CHINO (CBSLA.com) — A school board voted Monday night in favor of appealing a judge's ruling that banned prayer at meetings. After the 3-2 ...

School Board Plans To Fight Judge's Order That ... - CBS Los Angeles
losangeles.cbslocal.com/.../school-board-plans-to-fight-judges-order-
that- banned-prayer-at-meetings
Mar 3, 2016 ... Members of a local school board were under fire by angry parents Thursday after voting to keep fighting to include prayer at their meetings.

Begin forwarded message:

From: estherleon <estherleon@estherleon.com
Date: September 6, 2016 12:16:14 PM PDT
To: newsroom@wavepublication.com
Subject: GRATITUDE BUDDIE CIRCLE TO BE IMPLEMENTD IN ALL SCHOOLS

  Subject: Fwd: GRATITUDE BUDDIE CIRCLE TO BE IMPLEMENTD IN ALL SCHOOLS...Cantor Estherleon Schwartz a solution to help dispel antisemistism...
  Subject: GRATITUDE BUDDIE CIRCLE TO BE IMPLEMENTD IN ALL SCHOOLS

I am keeping my Papa:s promise when he threw me over the barb wired fence in 1944, Nazi:s chasing us, he looked to the heavens and said
 "save my daughter and she will always serve you"...

2016...IT IS OUR CHILDREN THAT WILL BRING ABOUT HARMONY, UNITY AND PEACE...in a peaceful way

History was made when one atheist argued that prayer in schools was unconstitutional and the Supreme Court agreed. Prayer in schools ended in 1962.

Now 2014, NOT the Supreme Court but the children have the opportunity to make their own history by "repealing" that decision. Not by reinstating prayer, but by starting a movement to replace it with a implemented program of beginning each school day with a Gratitude Circle before class starts, givng each child to share what they are grateful for (as seen in video below). They become buddies. One school at a time, and hopefully soon to be part of the morning school curriculum all over the nation.

This will help dispel bullying, discrimination and anti-semtisium. Children become school buddies and grow up caring and protecting one another. Giving a child a chance to express what they are grateful for in the morning before class starts leads to a good start for the day, gratitude feeds attitude for the rest of the day, for the rest of one's life. A simple morale teaching tool that leads to "in service work", to do good, instead of joining gangs...a moment of reverence, of oneness...And the child that never participates needs attention, not to wait until anger and rejection turns to violence and shootings, you know what I mean.

I, Cantor Estherleon Schwartz, am a face and voice, part of History and have been invited to schools to share my story of the Holocaust and how I survived. My presentation is with actual footage.. This is part of History.. PS...in Saudia Arabia, they took out all negation teachings towards hate. Just imagine Gratitude Buddies becoming Pin Pals thru school system in America. WOW...My friend, this is the month of miracles, I beleive in miracles.

"Who am I?"

Yes, all this on my mind
and sharing on Friday, close to,
of course, it's almost Shabbos, The Sabbath.
The heavens open up and the angels come down
and bless your wishes when you light the candles,
for Harmony and Peace for all God's Children.
I felt heard and did whatever I was guided to do,
in action and documentation...
writing these pages.
Who am I?
Kindly understand,
I am just a girl that was born
in times of slaughter and survived.
I am now a grown up girl with two children
and four grandchildren
and love dogs and humanity,
meaning all God's People...
And like when I was a Mommy
when my kids were little,
I tried to fix all their boo-boos.
So when there is a problem in the world to fix,
Mommy kicks in.
Meanwhile I do what I can
and do my very, very best
and let God do the rest.

I felt good about what I so far wrote
in these last few pages,
as I do want to wrap it up…
I called Ivor, as I do
to share what I write,
feeling excited and happy.
He knows me, I think
after over 20 years of spiritual,
creative partnership and he said,
"Aren't you are repeating yourself about the Sabbath?"
My inner response was,
"Dude, the Sabbath for all peoples
to gather, light candles, feast, and pray
cannot be shared enough times
on pages over and over in my a book,
until there is Harmony and Peace…
The Sabbath speaks to your soul
and lights up the world, temporarily broken…
Especially on The Sabbath, celebrated all over the world,
shared with all God's people…
brings their, your light, and gives Hope…

Dude!

Ivor, just maybe from now on...
it's me and God,
I shall call upon for affirmation.

Words that sting
Words that burn
Words that destroy
The gentle Heart
Of a being
A kind meaning word
Or none at all
Would be better
Than the words
That steal the breath
Of one
If not all

Monday January 15, 2024

Thinking about Destiny, feeling sad.
Always so wonderful,
missing our conversations.
Having the best hot chocolate
with homemade yummy whipping cream
at the Peninsula Hotel in Beverly Hills.
She is so informed.
So ahead of times…
Like my dear friend Adam…
when I asked him,
as a gifted astrologer beyond the moon and stars,
"What's your take on this life?"
and he quoted,
"Astrology is a valuable reflection of God's Creation,
but …He is above all of His Creation."
Blessed am I to have such friends I believe in…
what they think,
and always especially Adam and
TEARS OF GRATITUDE.
Ivor picking up the phone immediately,
and saying, "Hi,"
and me who knows very little about Astrology,
curious to know more from Adam.
You see, I and others have seen him
according to his gift in Astrology,
having resolved cold cases
and especially befriending my son.

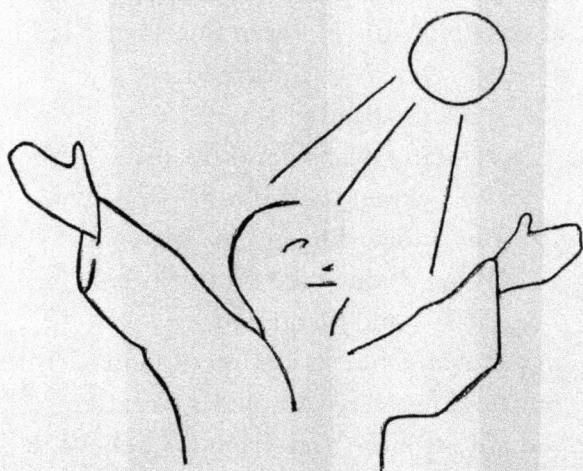

January 17th, 2024

So my friends, here I am
sitting on my balcony,
listening to the birds whistling
and I whistle back in-between
my three zips of coffee…
And then the daily saga continues…
Sure enough my lucky day,
Destiny calls and says, "I miss us,"
and I said, "Me tooo".
And Ivor, well, Ivor said he may write
a 1000 page book about me and him…
Oh well, "Never say never,"
as written in my other sequels.
And now, I'm good with me,
"Done did it"
and hopefully now not wake up
in the middle of the night and think,
"What page am I on?"
It was all worth it
to have a chance to once again,
bring you briefly up to date on my daily sagas.

Dear Friends,
These are off the top from my gut
so far right this minute
things that matter to me.
And expect the unexpected.

And now my readers,
what really matters to you?
I mean what really, really matters to you?
Take time to ponder in calmness
and the world will stand still and listen
and then with God's help,
a refreshed moral code that has drifted away
will be resurrected...

Really matters

friends that care
thru their
actions

Intimate wishes to share with God
your most intimate wishes and privacy

creating your sacred space

Prayer and lots of water

not being constipated

*Thank you Stevie Wonder for your lyrics
and the everlasting wonderful connections
by Alexander Graham Bell
that we stay connected
at any given moment.*

A phone call to say
"I just called to say?)

Thoughts become things.
(from the Universe, TUT).

you making your day good

*Morning, noon and
night...and in between*

*praying on behalf for
others that need your
essence in prayers...you*

Grow your own...
and witness birth that will nurture you

*healthy food that nurtures
your body and mind*

Gratitude before any meal and yummy snacks...

grace before eating

so helpful for healing and hope…
And building lasting friendships

joining a Bible study group

*Volunteering helps to get to know
what matters when feeling lost.*

Donating to children's hospitals

Can be
the best medicine…

Listening, just listening

*Staying connected
with Joy
day by day
until next Shabbos*

*Shabbos preparation
starting on Wednesdays*

(secret)
add DILL, DILL, DILL
and
matzoh ballls

Homemade blessed
chicken soup

a stranger no longer waiting…
your smile has given them hope

Acknowledge the homeless or a stranger walking by

In your brain,
in your heart,
on your tongue…

In-gratefulness all day long

Got my natural "high"

3 zips of cup of Coffee
in the morning

still searching

to find at last,
a mattress and pillow
to rest my soul

"and so it shall be"…

to sing again
thru the clouds
and reach the heavens
while still searching
what really, I mean
what really, really,
I mean really,
what matters to me
at this stage in my life
facing Mortality...

I miss my singing voice.
All in my first book,
Tears of Stone and my Deal with God…
Before I say "bye, bye for now,"
just a little feeling,
we will meet again,
a gut feeling,
and I go with one of my gifts from God
"my gut feelings".
Somewhere out there,
I'll be there,
looking upward or downward,
singing away onto you.
You will know it's me.

Hi, hang with me,
still searching
what really,
I mean what really,
really matters.
I mean what really,
really really matters

Yes,
this is what really,
really, really
matters to me
- my family.

*The personal relationship
with God and people*

...and

Mucho thank yous and blessings to my **Lionel**
for your words "done"
when I needed something asap
to create and print.

Thank you my friends at **Starbucks**
for making my pour over coffee
with so much love with extra foam.

To my **Kristin**, **Travis**, **Sean** of *Sirens Salon* in L.A.
for all your immediate attention
when I wonder in and you say,
"OK. I have 30 min, what color
do you want your bangs today?"

And to **Delilah**, my assistant,
who never fails me thru thick and thin
to reach all of you
my sending out the information.
Yah, she was inivited to be a student at UCLA.

To **Richard**, your daily thoughts
in the morning message
really mean alot to me…e

AND to all in the neighborhood for your *hello's*
and letting me pet your dogs
and sometime give them a homemade cookie
from the **Dog Bakery**
at the Farmers Market at the Grove
And all the care from **C/S**…

Without Michael's creativity
and lots of sensibility
and lots of professional experience
and wise input formatting my books,
there would be no book.
For real, as I could not explain
my vision to someone
unknowen to me,
"my style"…(whatever that is,
can't even explain it to me)

And my Rickie,
aka Rivka…
Always wishing me "golden dreams".
In Hebrew…
is when I fall
asleep

AND to Ivor Pyres...
Over 20 years I know him,
I really, really know him
as a caring, devoted loving man of God.
He has been my right and left hand
in my emotional and creative adventures
and my singing partner in duet.
His essence is in all my books,
as he has been my rock
and beleiver in me since we met
at the American Film Institute
and became spiritual friends.
I wish a friend like him onto everyone.

Once again and again,
morning, noon and night
and in-between,
I lift my eyes and heart upward
and give "a billion thank yous
for this most beautiful God-given green earth."

Everything matters in the moment.

There is something greater

Above and around us

There is something bigger

That helps us and guides us

Through our darkness

The intellectual

The spiritual quest

A cause and effect

Be in awe, seek, become

The child of inspiration

The child of poems

The child of songs

The joyous child

Of God

(*reprinted from 'Tears of Stone and My Deal with God' by Estherleon)

Well here is my response.

When all is said and done, when all of the cards are on the table when you are floating from above...what really mattered?

It is almost impossible to call all of the shots. To decide for ourselves what were the reasons why. Was it worth it? What was just a waste?

What matters it must be is... LIFE. In order for something to be true it must persist. What is any of it if no one is experiencing it anyway? It is "the whole enchilada" the big story and the greatest love.

It is all of it. The answer to this enigma must be a big resounding EVERYTHING.

But how is it? How can everything be the answer? Well in my opinion... it is.

We live in a multi-verse where nothing is wasted. Not stardust not information, not energy. Absolutely everything contributes to this whole. With this judgment of design into account. I conclude that it must be that; every breath is like a snowflake with its breathtaking beauty of design. Every person, every smile, every baby's warm hug, every cat that is silly. Every business deal, every crushing defeat. All of the wonderful dreams of adolescence, every first kiss and butterflies enchanting visit.

It all matters

That is why it is here.

Was here

And will be here!

The thing to delight in is that it was all given to every one of us as we struggle, love, and cry our way through existence. It is good to remember that this was created with us forever

intertwined. We are the threads in the tapestry. Our actions are the victories and the horrors. We get to be in G-Ds mind his everlasting eternity. We share as a part of it all. So in the words of Estherleon Schwartz " Look up" and "give gratitude" for this gift because everything matters. After all, it is our beautiful one-of-a-kind gift. Maybe if we do look up we might see G-D's message in the clouds might say...Made especially for you...
Love G-D.

Destiny
author of inspiring works manifesto

~

When Esther asked me to write a excerpt in her book about what was important to me, the trite overused word kindness appeared, which apparently, I have been noticing for awhile, seems to be on hiatus, and what of it associates, compassion, honor integrity goodness, and courage. All the words, thoughts, I have seen in poetry books. As a child of immigrants there wasn't much poetic about that. I would listen to a commentator when I was about 5, just to hear at the end, a poem he would read I was enthralled. The poems would fill my childhood senses, ah, to be able to speak up for what is right there used to be an absolute, a cliche that set you on path of doing right in the universe.

People turn to many avenues of safety to help them navigate this difficult life. I turned to poetry, when I felt especially sad, I would read a few lines from a poem, that said. " I hear the croaking's of dismay the dark predictions of the weak. I find myself perused by care, no matter what the end I seek" when read, I felt I wasn't alone there were others that felt the same, and " this too shall pass away". There was always hope at the end

Now, getting to now

I find discontent, rage, people off balance, inconsolable, doing the unspeakable, and committing, act of violence, where are the people supposed the take control. Didn't we put people in positions of power? that had jobs that names, and office's that were elected to negoiate and have to know how to do something, anything that works.

Instead: Now we get to what really, rally really bothers me, as well as important. Our lives, and the people in charge of our lives.

We are consumed with misrepresentation, blatant lies, they

have masters, doctorates, plaques of honor, and we are eaten up by their effortless, practiced words, their warm and folksy blab, behind the cloak of decency, we are taken in as they ramble on with their flowery talk, and thus do nothing.

They dismiss, then ignore, then have town-hall meetings, symposiums, act, bill's measures, proposition, all to look like they are doing something... So, they blame the migrants, the illegal's, the poor, the other billionaires, the criminal element, the homeless, is fodder for them. They fix nothing, and often it is not fixable. but, they go forward because they have a job with benefits.

I have met with gang members with more heart than those who seem to be in our country and local government.

This among other things, really, really bothers me and that is why everyone is crazed, from lack of integrity, honor, honesty, goodness, caring and it's working for them.

I would like to end this with a poem, I did not write. Oh, I didn't tell you. Life is like a poem it has rhythm, pulse, thought, balance, uplifting incite. You might want to try it sometime.

In men who men condemn as ill
I find so much of goodness still
In men who men pronounce divine,
I find so much of sin and blot, that I
Dare not, to draw the line,
Where God has not

Amy Schultz - activist

~

If someone asked me What is fundamental in this life?
What is the most valuable thing? It is not a thing. Sharing
with others. Caring for others in this life is the most essen-
tial way to live. It is not only fundamental but is our most
basic human nature. To give is to receive. . To not know
this is to not know yourself and your truest nature. Nothing
will ever feel as good as knowing that your efforts helped
someone else in need. Always be kind. Always have com-
passion. FOR yourself and for others and life will be easier
and more filled with love.
There you go!
Love

Rachel Schultz (sister of Amy Schultz)

~

What I REALLY care about!

I care about my family and my friends' well being

I care about my family, friends and our ability to pursue our dreams, which in itself, meaning the journey, provides not only purpose and inspiration, but also the endorphins created that fuel our well being.

I care about trying to "buy back my time", to do the things I want to, have never done and want to do again, so that life doesn't just pass me by, so that when looking back I can say that I had the privilege of doing the things most important to me.

I care about finding time and/or being able to help people because it IS better to give than receive and there's immense joy in that.

I care about using the gift I was given of being a "Healer" to help heal people and animals because I know that my energy is VERY powerful and I wish there were more of me to give and I had more resources because I know that I would inspire huge change within people, communities and more, but we only have one life.

I care about leaving a better planet for my grandchildren and the future generations.

I care about people

I care about animals

I care about feelings

I care about me

I care about sharing my music with the world because music is a healer

I care about making a difference

I care about what Esther is doing to inspire and create change.

Rick Virag

~

Dear Esther,

Here it goes:
What really, really, reallllly matters to me:
People being kind to one another. The ability to listen without thinking of what you're going to say next. Children growing up with positive self-esteem so they can create families, cities, states, countries that that work for the greater good, not work for their egos!
Helping men, women and children learn healthy ways to conflict resolution without calling anyone names or blaming anyone.
To help create a world that is healthy in mind, body and sprit so that we can create and build for the present and future, while preserving the legacy of the past.

Ruth Klein,
CEO, Expert Celebrity Branding
"Everything Brands & Books"

~

The thing that matters most to me are many things, having something to do and having something to look forward to. Having a good friend, and having someone to love. Having a sense of self, with love and empathy for others.

Richard Donohue

~

Dear Family of Man/Woman...

WE are all in this together. We breathe and are fortunate if we can, we live in Peace, Love, and Hope, and fortunate if we can... let's all love one another. Let's www.pausetheworldforpeace.org at least starting on September 21, 2024, from Times Square, join us and pray from that moment on that Peace becomes our way of life for ALL. Talking about all, we share with you our movie: Woodstock Forever: Peace, Love & HOPE. A movie that for ALL represents once again the Good in Humankind and our Animal and Plant King and Queen Doms. WE ARE ONE WITH ALL. We love you and appreciate you, Cantor Esther, you have been an inspiration for me for many years, you walk the talk and you also have a beautiful voice to go along with your kind spirit for life that you share with ALL.. We need your energy and this book shares your movement for Goodness, it is an honor to join you.

Reverend Paul Sladkus, All Faiths and Spiritual Founder:
www.goodnewsplanet.TV
www.youtube.com/goodnewsbroadcast
www.pausetheworldforpeace.org

~

To be continued...

expect the unexpected